Realistic coloring books for adults

COLORING BOOKS FOR ADULTS RELAXATION

LANDSCAPE

Copyright 2020 by

Sabella Blossom

More coloring books by Sabella Blossom
Available on AMAZON.

Birds in the Flower Garden
A calming therapy and anti-stress coloring book

Sabella Blossom
birds and blooms coloring book

More coloring books by Sabella Blossom
Available on AMAZON.

More coloring books by Sabella Blossom
Available on AMAZON.

Joyous Moments
AN ANTI STRESS COLORING BOOK FOR ADULTS

Hand drawn coloring book
Sabella Blossom